# GAVIN TURK

Gavin Turk rose to prominence in the early 1990s during the so-called 'young British artists' phenomenon: a wave of media interest provoked by an ambitious generation of artists with a flair for self-promotion. Turk's thoughtful, visually striking work gained him a reputation as an artist who questioned the nature and values of identity, pop culture, and art itself.

Turk was born in Guildford, near London, in 1967. By 1989 he had completed three years at Chelsea School of Art and entered the Royal College of Art, London. The way that he left the Royal College two years later made Turk an art world cause célèbre: for his graduation exhibition Turk presented 'Cave' [p.9], a whitewashed studio, empty save for an English Heritage-style blue plaque commemorating the artist's two-year stint in the space. Senior members of staff convinced themselves they were the butt of some joke they didn't get and refused Turk his MA degree – the first time this had ever happened. However, many visitors, including the young art dealer, Jay Jopling, recognized the artwork as a serious, multi-layered installation with a knowing take on art history. The piece brought Turk critical acclaim and academic notoriety in equal measure.

Within two years Turk put on a precocious retrospective: 'Collected Works 1989-1993', in conjunction with Jopling. In 1995 his work featured in 'Young British Artists IV', one of The Saatchi Gallery's influential exhibitions. Also in London, 1997 saw his work in both the Hayward Gallery's British sculpture survey 'Material Culture' and the Royal Academy of Arts' controversial exhibition 'Sensation', which later toured globally. In 1998 Turk presented 'The Stuff Show', a solo exhibition at the South London Gallery, and in 2002 The New Art Gallery Walsall, UK, hosted his 'Copper Jubilee' exhibition. Outside the commercial art world, Turk initiates anarchic, artist-led street fairs and events in London, where he currently lives and works.

# INTERVIEW

DAVID BARRETT **You first came to prominence in 1991 with your blue-plaque artwork, 'Cave' [p.9]. It was widely seen as announcing the death of this fictional self that you had created. Is that how you saw it?**

GAVIN TURK No; the whole 'dead artist' thing started because a woman who visited the exhibition thought that one of the students, Gavin Turk, had gone off to the Gulf War earlier that year and been killed. She thought that the other students had made this plaque to commemorate him. I can understand her logic, because the postcard that I had accompanying the installation was a piece called 'Window' [p.13], which showed me wearing a beret against a Union Jack background. This was based on a cover of the British tabloid, The Sun, at the time, which was specifically about the Gulf War.

But the work was actually much simpler than that. It was about being based in Kensington, in London, at that time and wondering where it might take you if you did have a successful career as an artist. I guess that was the biographical element, or the bit about the fictional artist 'Gavin Turk'. But it was also a technical piece in a way, because I wanted to find a way of exhibiting just empty space, showing – in inverted quotes – 'nothing'. I suppose I was thinking about [the French artist] Yves Klein's ideas of purity: he would make pure blue paintings of the void. But I wanted to show something purer than pure form – that is, show the space itself. The plaque was a device that allowed me to do that.

**A kind of excuse for the empty space?**

It let me exhibit the context of the artwork, rather than an actual object. I was very interested in museums at the time. The Royal College of Art is right in the heart of London's so-called 'Albertopolis' [the dense cluster of museums in Kensington that had been the pet project of Queen Victoria's husband, Prince Albert]. So I spent a lot of time in museums while at college and got interested in the way they classify things. They developed these methods of specifying what was and what wasn't important, what was and what wasn't of value, what was and what wasn't desired or acquired.

**You actually worked at the Victoria and Albert Museum for a while didn't you?**

Yeah. As a slide technician, when I was a student. All that stuff was quite an influence on my work at the time. But I think that when you move from studio to studio you pick up different sets of stimuli from your environment. Like now; this studio is on one of central London's major roads and one of my most recent pieces has been 'Nomad' [p.36] – a figure lying in the street, not too dissimilar to what you see outside.

**What other ideas did you pick up from museums?**

This idea of something being fixed in the world. Taking something from the fluctuating sea of culture and life that we know as 'the present', and then fixing it so that it can communicate in a different time and place. It's the bits that get kept that we use to construct our histories, and it's our histories that we use to take a bit of a stab at understanding the present.

The more 'museumalized' something gets – that is, the more polished it is, or the greater the number of framing devices that surround it – the more these things get in the way of the object that you're actually trying to look at. And that happens in all walks of life, not just museums.

**Is your use of signatures** [p.10] **part of the same exploration of framing devices?**

There are various points about the signature that interest me, one of which is the idea of painting a signature, rather than signing it. So it's a picture of a signature, rather than an actual signature.

**The purpose of the signature, to authenticate some other content, is lost—**

—and the signature becomes the content. But in some ways the signature is the content already: for example, if you have two similar paintings by one artist, one with a signature and one without, the one with the signature is always of more value, economically speaking. And yet the paintings may be landscapes, say, which have been realized through the skill of the painter, who has carefully created an illusion of depth and space. And then this signature gets scrawled across the bottom right-hand corner, absolutely destroying any illusion of space that had been so masterfully set up. The attempt by the artist to make an out-of-context appearance in the artwork actually ends up defacing the picture. So it's as if the signature is the real subject of the painting anyway, and the picture is secondary, like you're not supposed to look at it.

**Because the authenticated touch of the artist has become more important than the qualities of the work itself?**

The value of the signature is tied into the romantic notion of the artist-as-genius, where the hand of the artist literally has a Midas touch. That's something I definitely play with in my work. And the actual form of the signature in my work is important too. I've constructed my signature – the spacing of the letters, their shapes – so that it can be read within a history of signatures. And I have different signatures for different jobs. I don't sign letters in the same way I sign artworks; I've got an art signature and I've got a bank signature, and the two are quite separate. I've also been making signatures that are stamps: that is, not actually signatures at all – just the name.

**What about the idea of transformation? A lot of your works seem to have been taken through several forms.**

It's more a question of trying to reveal things external to the object. For example, I like taking an item through different stages, only for it to end up being exactly the same as it was to begin with. And yet it has still changed because your knowledge of it has changed. Like when [the French Surrealist and Dadaist artist] Marcel Duchamp introduced the readymade object to art – the object was perfectly ordinary but its reason for being had changed. The artwork was created through the shift in context. A transformation had certainly occurred, but not within the material of the object. It was purely mental; it was the viewer's consciousness of the object that had changed.

**But you often change the materials of your objects too, in an alchemical way. I guess that's also related to the artist's Midas touch that you mentioned earlier.**

That's true. One current project I'm working on involves casting bits of used chewing-gum in platinum. I like the idea of imbuing something that has a relationship with the body, but is also a waste object, with the value of a precious metal. Chewing-gum is interesting because it's so much about individual identity: used gum holds dental prints, fingerprints and saliva – which carries DNA. So a used piece of gum is a kind of forensic identification of the self. And yet formally the gum is identity-less; it has a sculptural form, but the form is created randomly [p.26]. It's the same meaningless form that full bin bags have, and I've used those in my work too [p.40].

**People stick used gum on posters – like graffiti tagging, which is also an assertion of identity.**

I am particularly keen on people sticking chewing-gum on posters. It's like a revenge for the visual pollution that marketing departments create. Sticking gum on the eyes of a model transforms the idealized figure into a surreal, nightmarish vision – exactly what we don't want to look like! It completely reverses the ad's effect.

**So identity plays a major role in your work?**

'Pop' [p.17] was one of my first works that dealt with identity. It's me dressed as Sid Vicious singing 'My Way'. But it's actually a Frank Sinatra song, so the question becomes, 'whose way is it?'

**Asserting the self while undermining it?**

Or asserting the wrong identity. We are given our identities from the outside: our identities are created through associations or similarities with other identities. There is a history of identities that we operate within, and we are understood through associations with the past. That's partly what 'Pop' is about.

**What about the form of your work? You often make very traditional art objects, although the ideas behind them might be radical.**

I've always liked the idea of making art that is quite pure, in so far as it is just stuff in space: good old-fashioned art. And I do consciously make it accessible – like my piece 'Death of Marat' [p.32]. This is based on Jacques-Louis David's painting of the same name. David was a leading figure in the French revolution at the end of the 18th century, but his painting style was incredibly conservative – it was based on Greek Classicism. The neo-classical style was a very popular, accessible style, and he used it to put forward revolutionary ideas. It doesn't have to be that way, of course; at the start of the 20th century the Russian avant-garde proposed a revolution of form to accompany the new ideas of the Russian revolution. But that can make the ideas doubly difficult for a general audience to understand.

**Your works frequently refer quite directly to pieces by other artists, don't they?**

There are a group of artists that I'm greatly inspired by and I quite often think, 'What a great piece of work – I wish I could make a work like that'. And so I might actively try to make a work that looks a bit like it, so the feelings of enjoyment that I get from my piece are similar to those that I got from the original work. It's a self-conscious homage, in a way.

**Do you worry that people might not recognize the references, if they're not familiar with art history?**

No, it just presents different levels of readings in a work. For example, when I use [the Italian Dadaist] Piero Manzoni in my work, on a general social level most people don't know who Manzoni is, and I don't think that matters. But I do think that his work has been very important and influential within art. And because of that I think people are aware of his work on a subconscious level, whether that's because they've actually seen copies of it, or whether it's because his work has inspired various other cultural artefacts in the world – such as advertising, or graphic design, or brand packaging. I believe his work has inspired enough creative people for some of its character to have seeped through into the broader visual culture. This is partly why people prefer older artworks to new art: on some level they are already familiar with older work because it has so influenced our visual culture.

I like the idea of working with subconscious registers. Take a work like 'Pop'; the pose that I used is just a compositional device. Now, the Andy Warhol reference that I was working from for the way the figure stands does get written about, but even if you didn't read anything about the pose, I still think you would have some sort of affinity with the way the figure is standing – as if you recognize that way of standing, as if that way of standing makes a kind of sense to you.

**Like 'pipe'** [p.12]**, with its position on the plinth relating to the pipe on the chair in the Vincent van Gogh painting?**

Yeah. That's a very esoteric reference, I know, but it gave me a way of composing the piece.

**And viewers might recognize the position, but not know why?**

They might just feel that it's in the right place, somehow. That work was also a tribute to [Belgian Surrealist] René Magritte's painting of a pipe, 'The Betrayal of Images', which was a picture about how you see pictures. That's a very important work to me; it's incredibly well-known and has influenced a lot of people, and it's become a total cliché. And I quite like the idea of dealing with clichés. I'm drawn to them because they are a point at which people make an agreement that something is right, and so everybody uses it. But because everybody is using it, it loses its specificity – its proper meaning – and actually becomes something you wouldn't want to use if you want to be clear. But in amongst all this lack of clarity there is still a truth, which is quite appealing.

**Pipes are clichéd objects too.**

Yeah. Blokes sitting around in the 1920s, deep in philosophical, contemplative reveries.

**I find your work contemplative – is this something you aim for?**

I hope that it is contemplative. I know there's a reactionary quality to the work – in so far as they're often traditional, figurative sculptures – but I hope that it isn't simply reactionary. I hope that the works have enough layers of ideas that viewers can keep finding new things within them.

**You once said that if you were on a desert island you wouldn't make art, which suggests that your work is about taking part in a cultural discussion, rather than self-expression.**

It is about dealing with yourself, but with your 'self' as a cultural self.

**So why do you make art?**

Why do I want to make art? That's a difficult one. It changes from day to day. Partly it's a response to seeing other art and enjoying it so much that I've wanted to give the same kind of enjoyment through making art. And also the flip-side of that, which is that I've seen so much disappointing art that I've felt that I've had to go and make the kind of art that I want to see. It's also because there's this whole rich history of art – an incredible project – and I want to make art so I can continue looking at and, in some small way, take part in that history.

This interview took place in October 2003 in the artist's studio on Charing Cross Road, London.

Additional interview material can be found at:
**www.newartupclose.com**

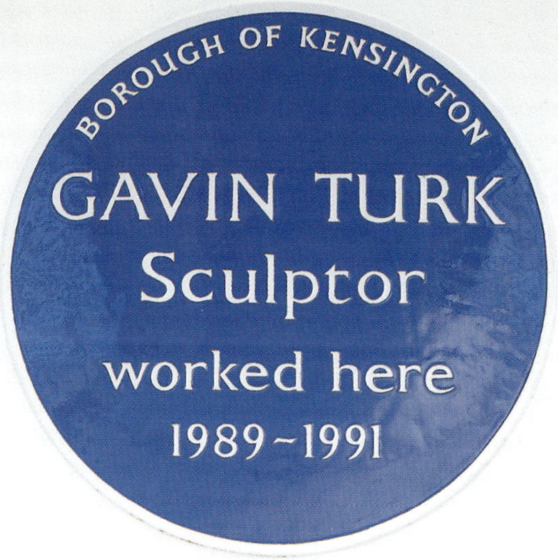

BOROUGH OF KENSINGTON
GAVIN TURK
Sculptor
worked here
1989~1991

**Cave (detail)**

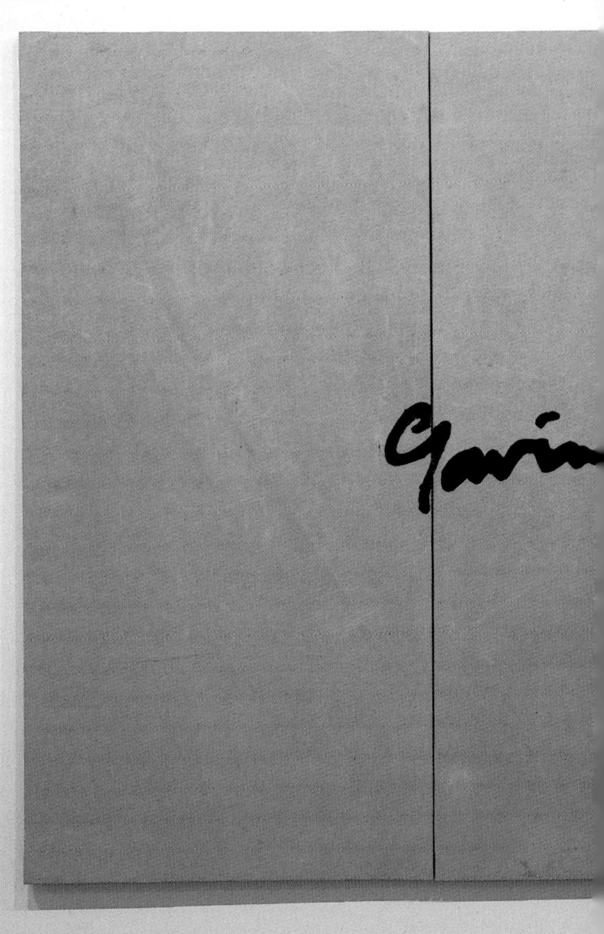


**Title**

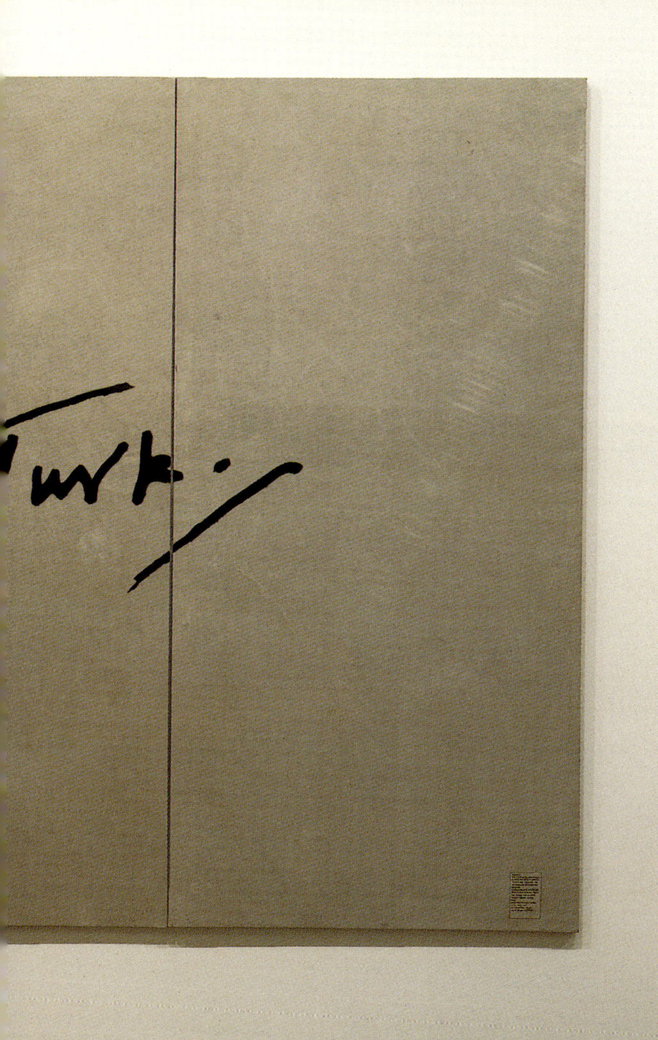
Turk

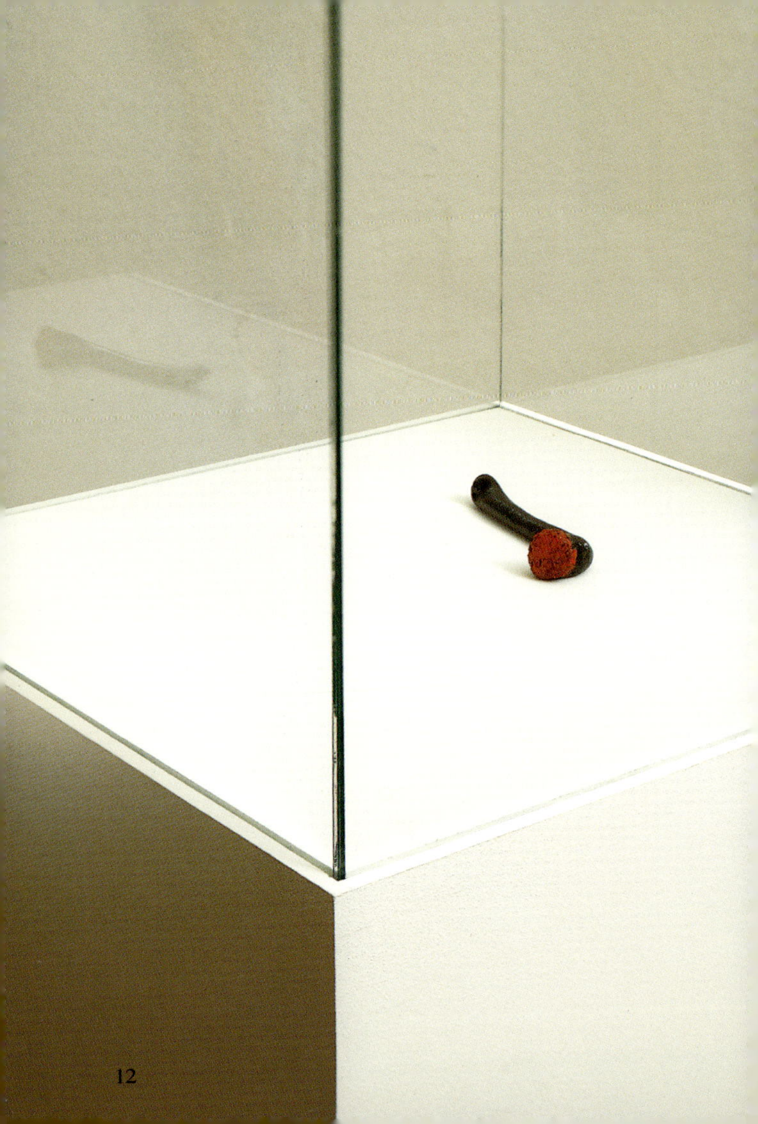

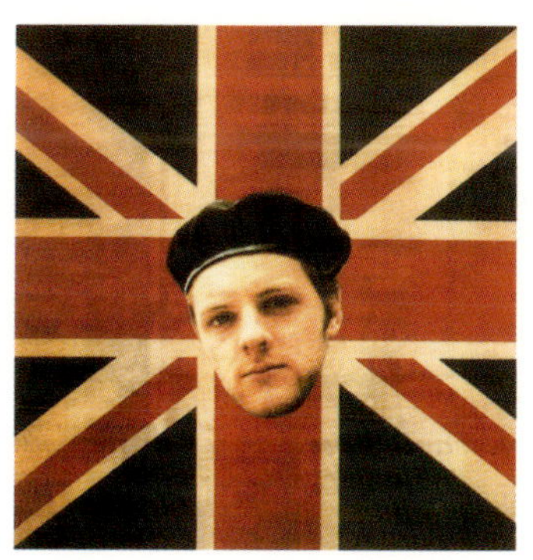

ABOVE **Window**
OPPOSITE **pipe (detail)**

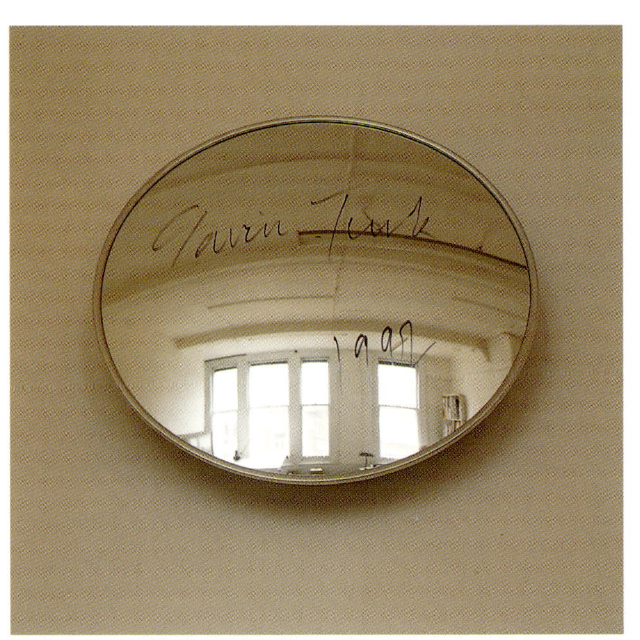

**Epiphany**

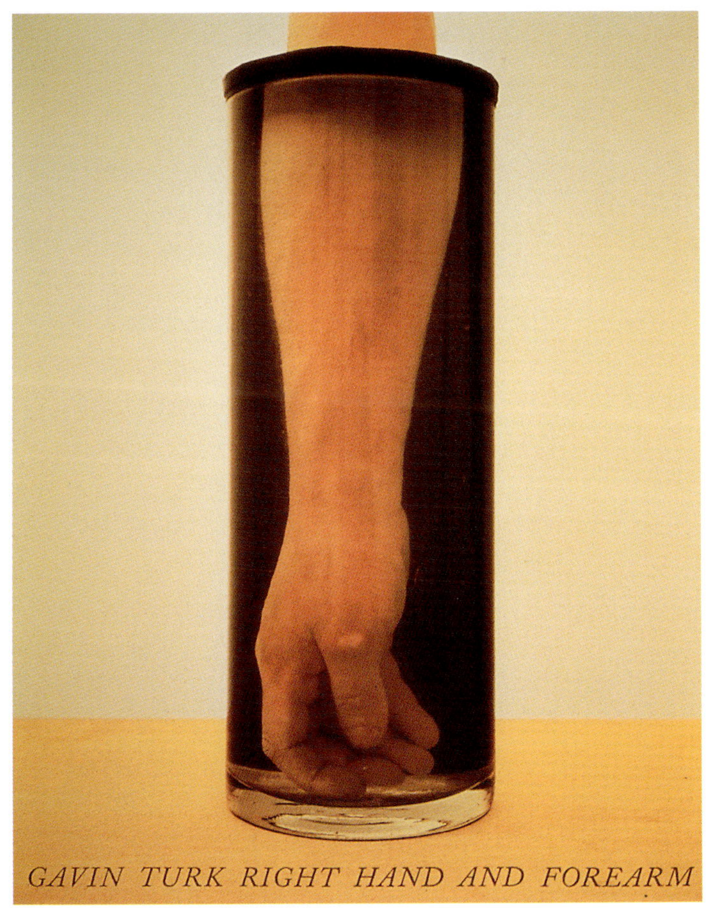


**Gavin Turk Right Hand and Forearm**

**Pop**

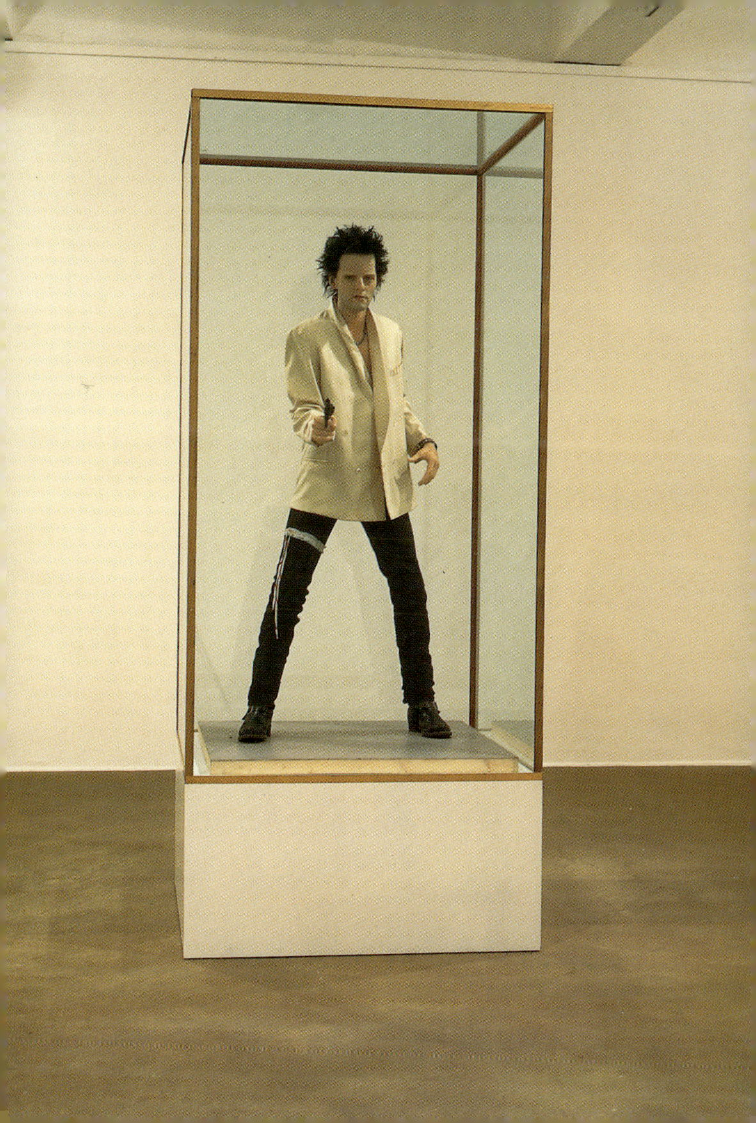

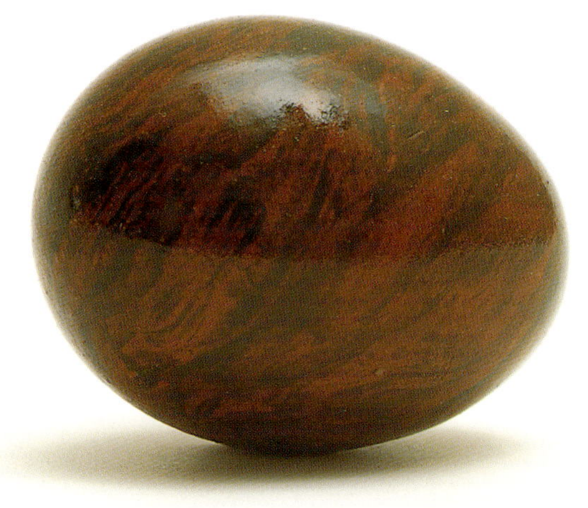

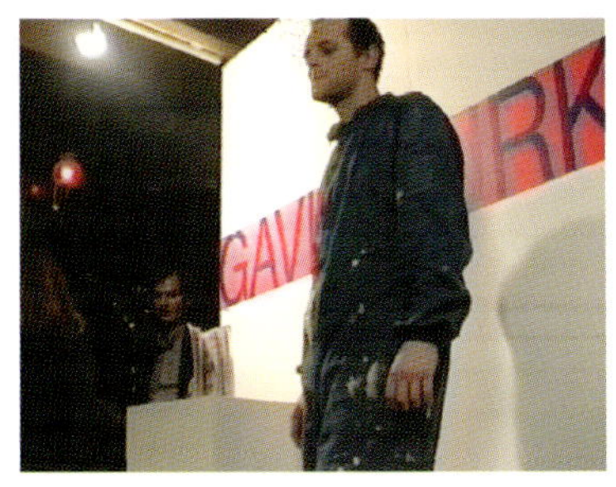

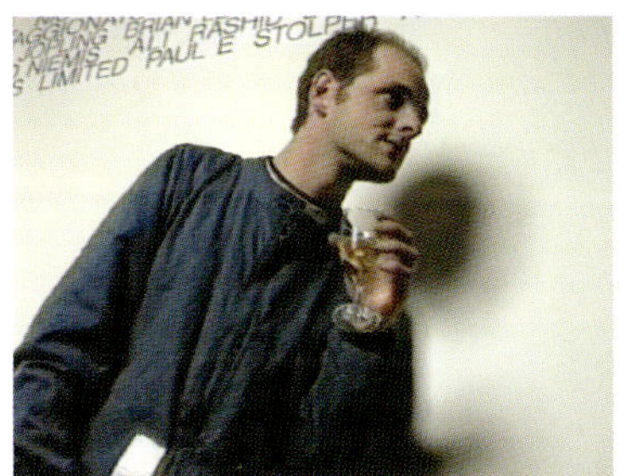

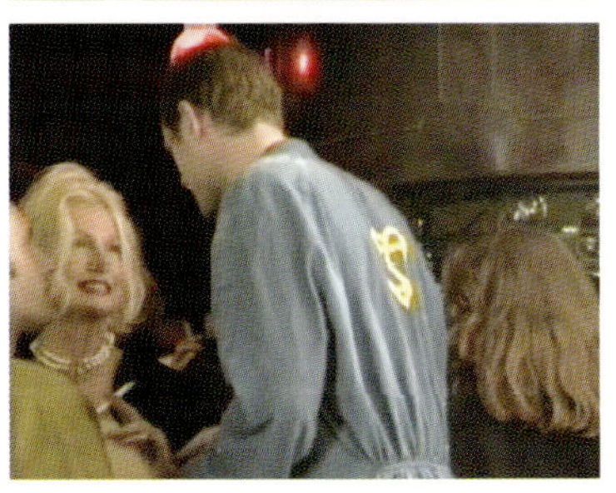

ABOVE **A Night Out with Gavin Turk (video stills)**
OPPOSITE **Briar Egg (detail)**

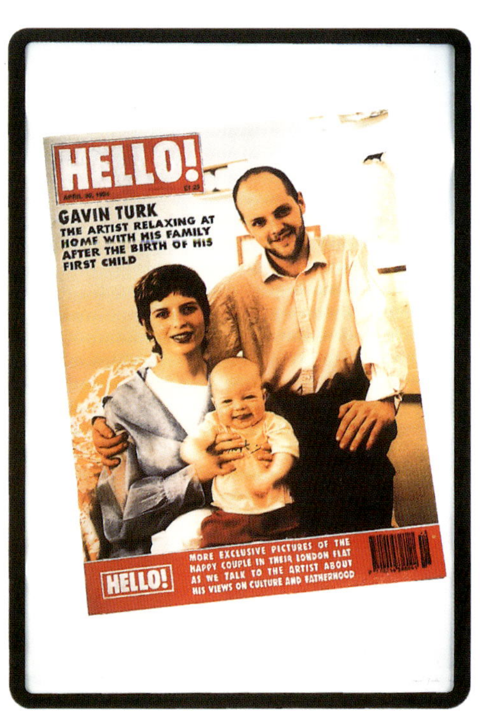


ABOVE **Identity Crisis**
OPPOSITE **The Spirit of Gavin Turk**

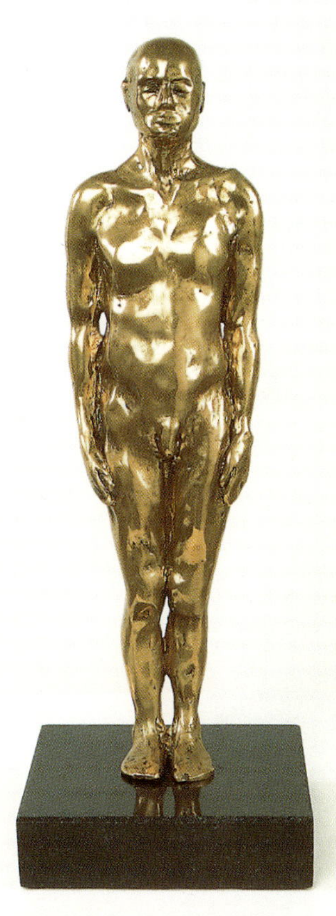

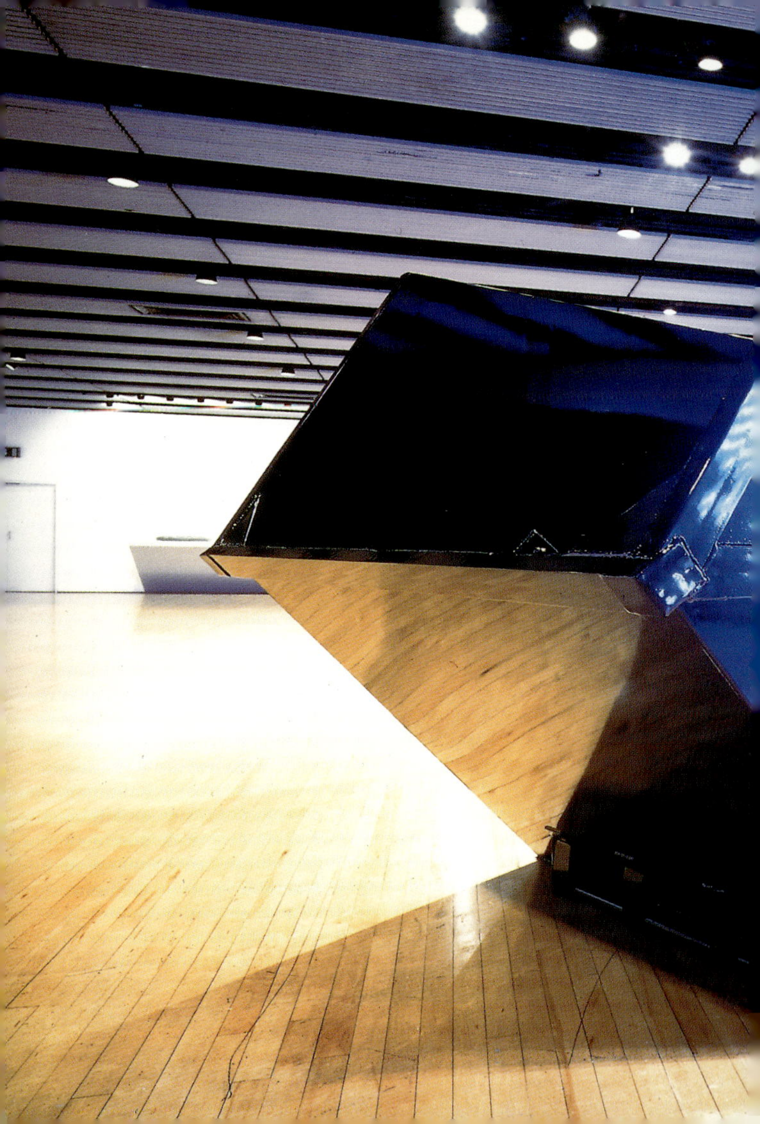

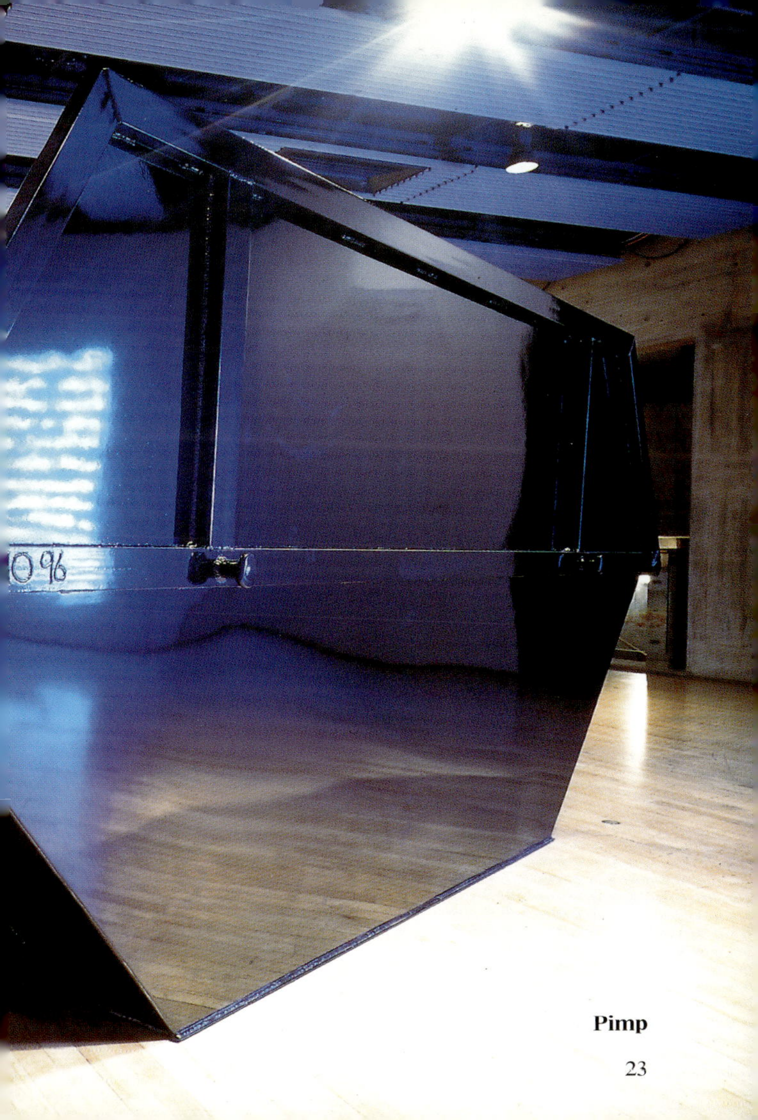


Pimp

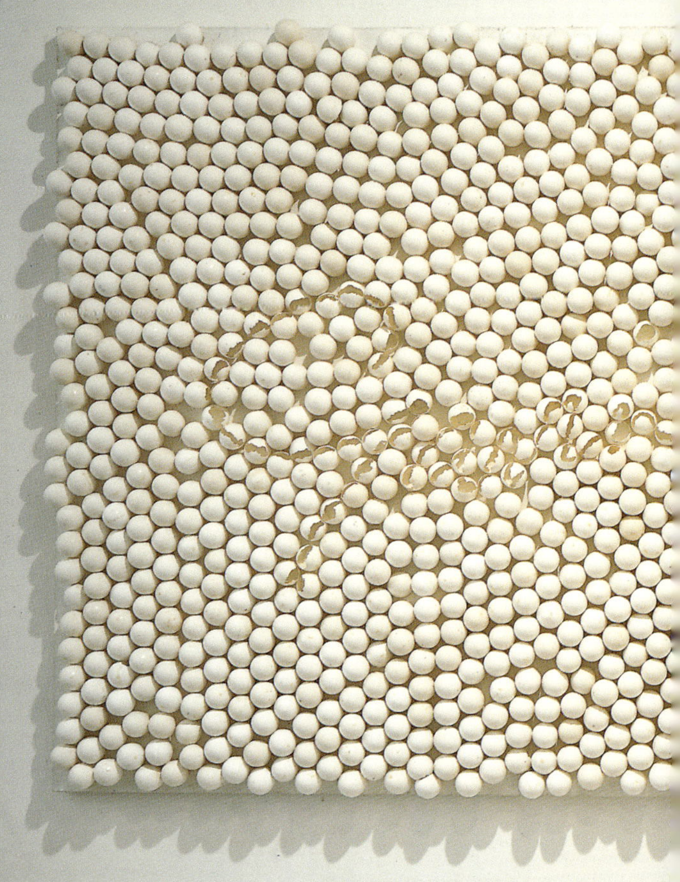

**One thousand, two hundred and thirty four eggs**

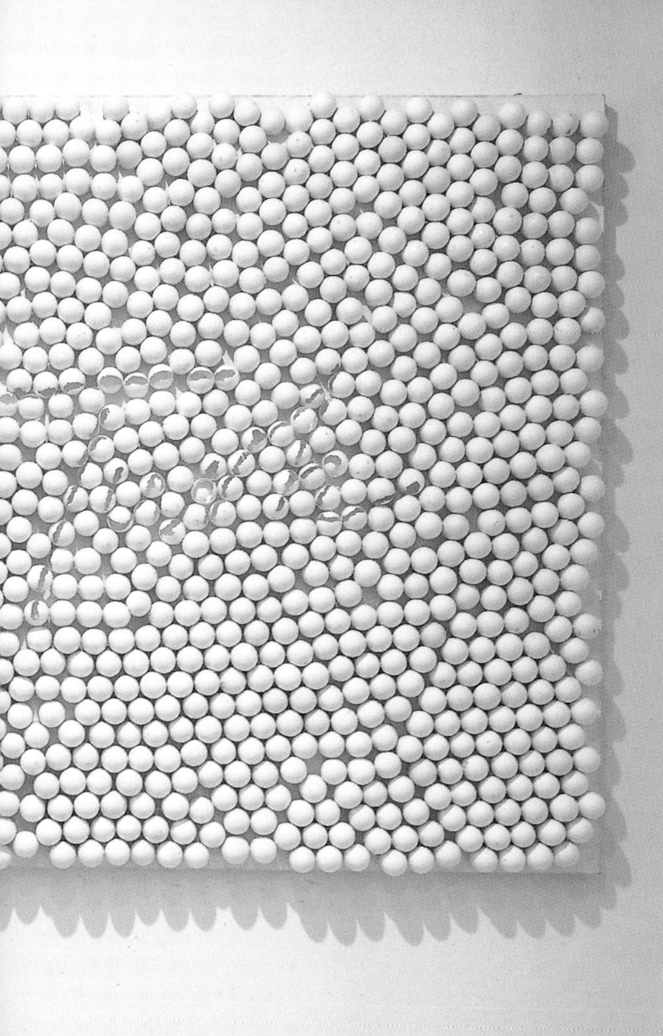

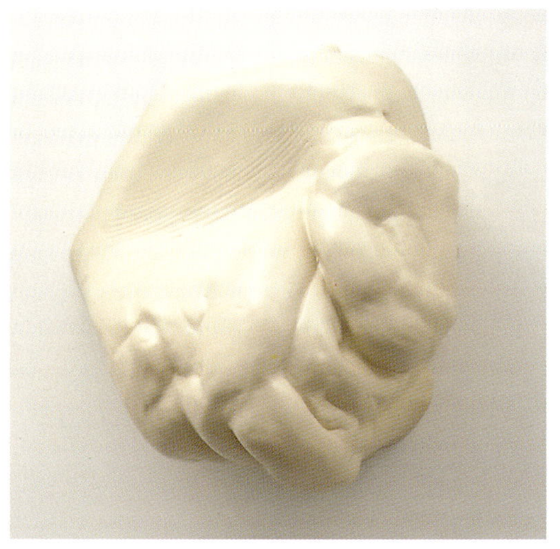

**PK2**

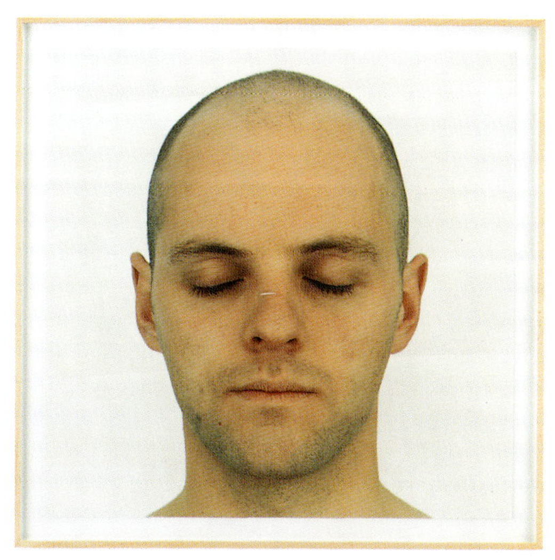

**Portrait of something that I'll never really see**

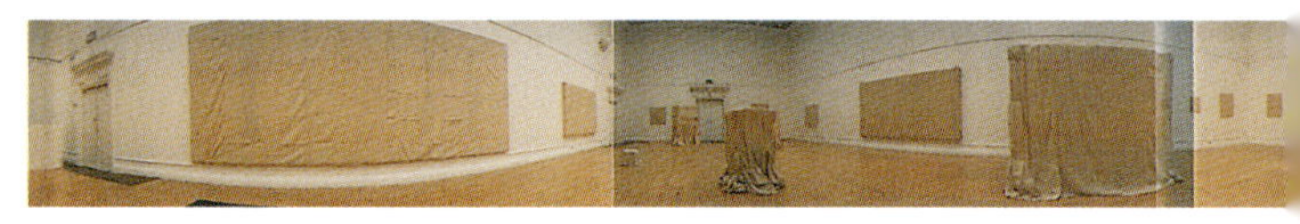

**Droste Effect**

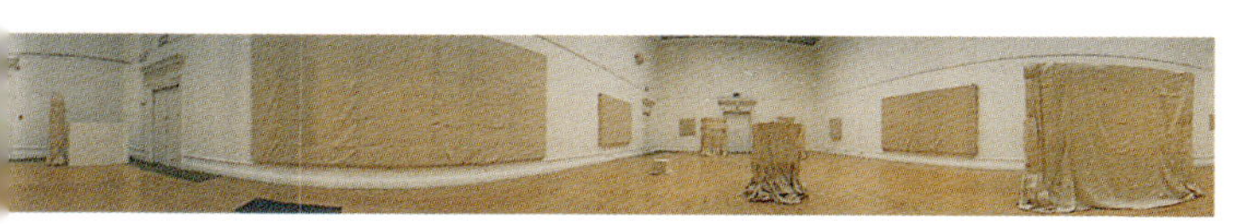

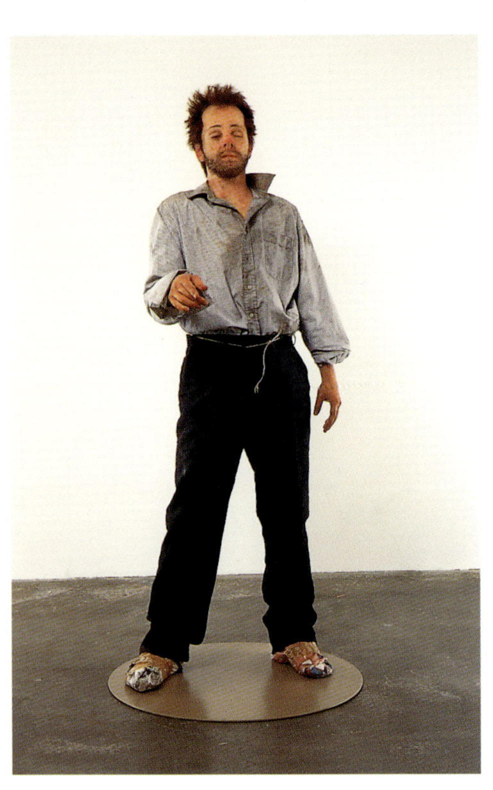

ABOVE **The Last Bum**
OPPOSITE **The Last Bum (detail)**

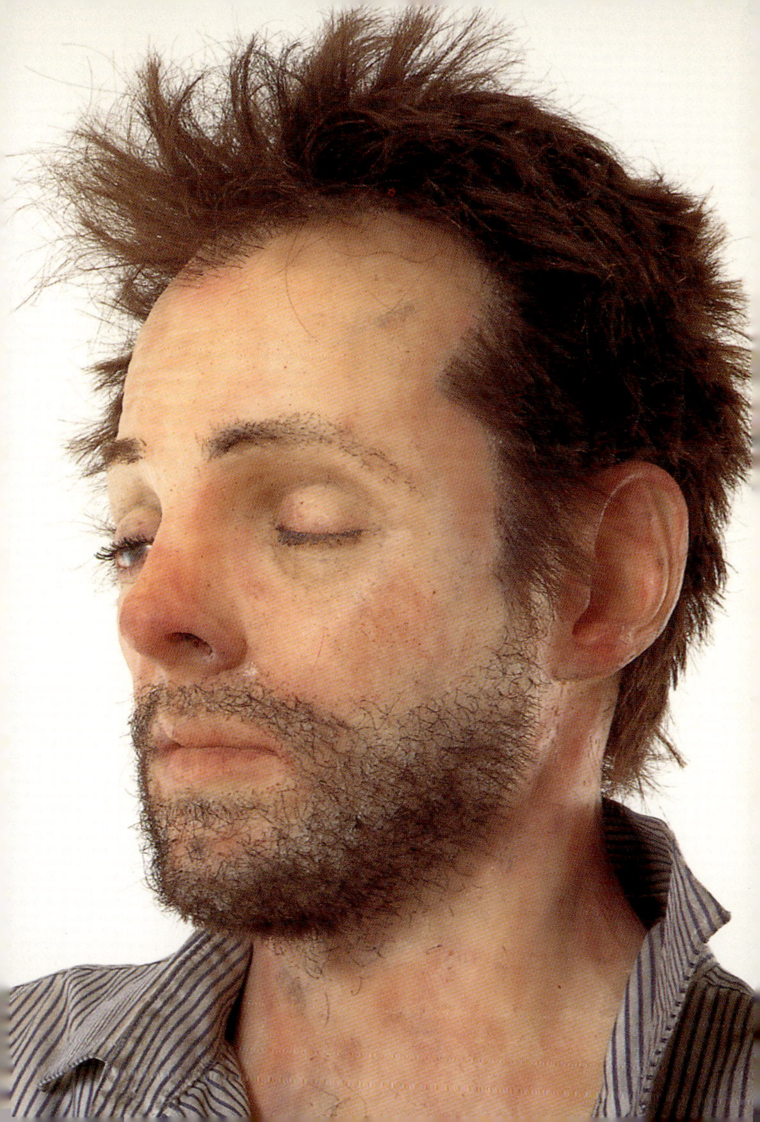

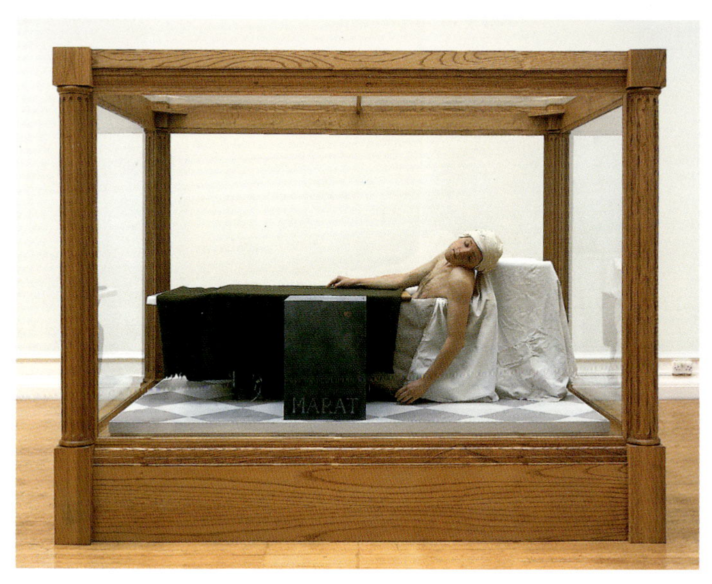


**Death of Marat**

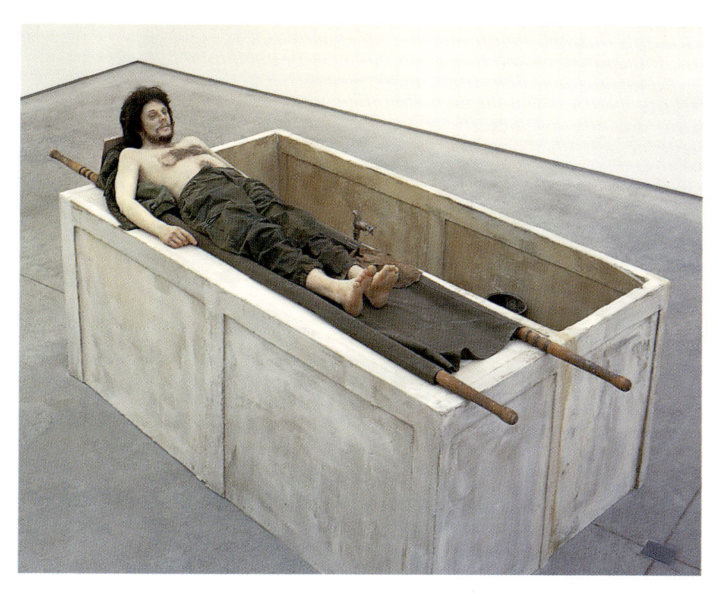

**Death of Che**

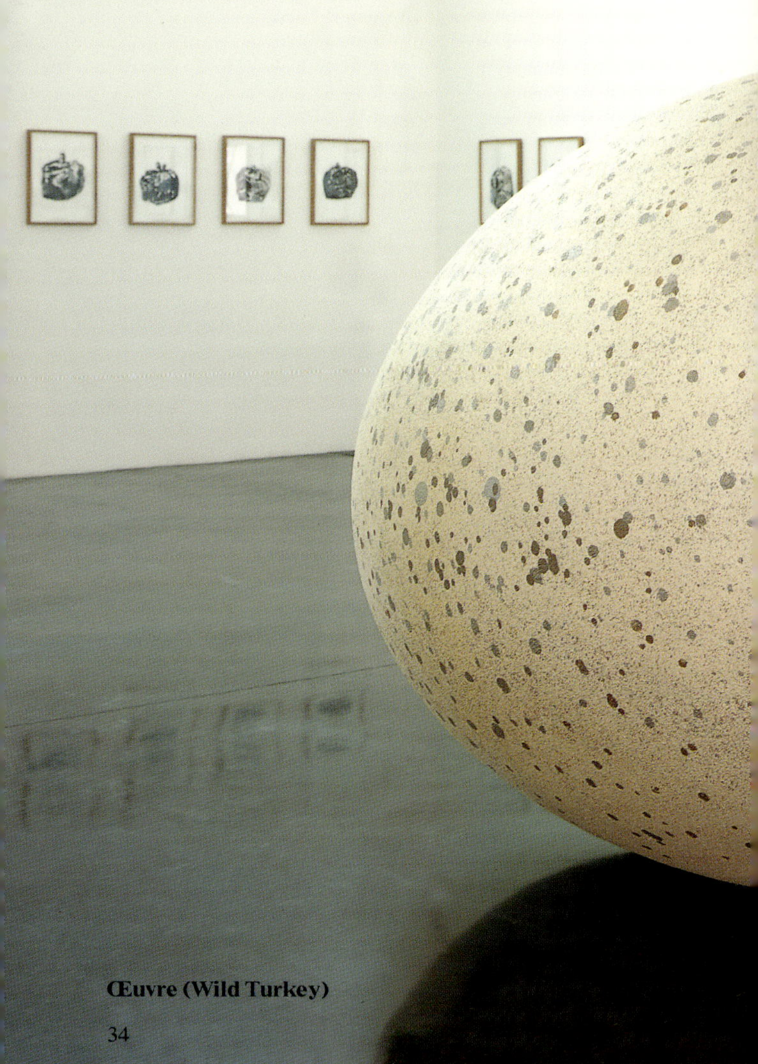

**Œuvre (Wild Turkey)**

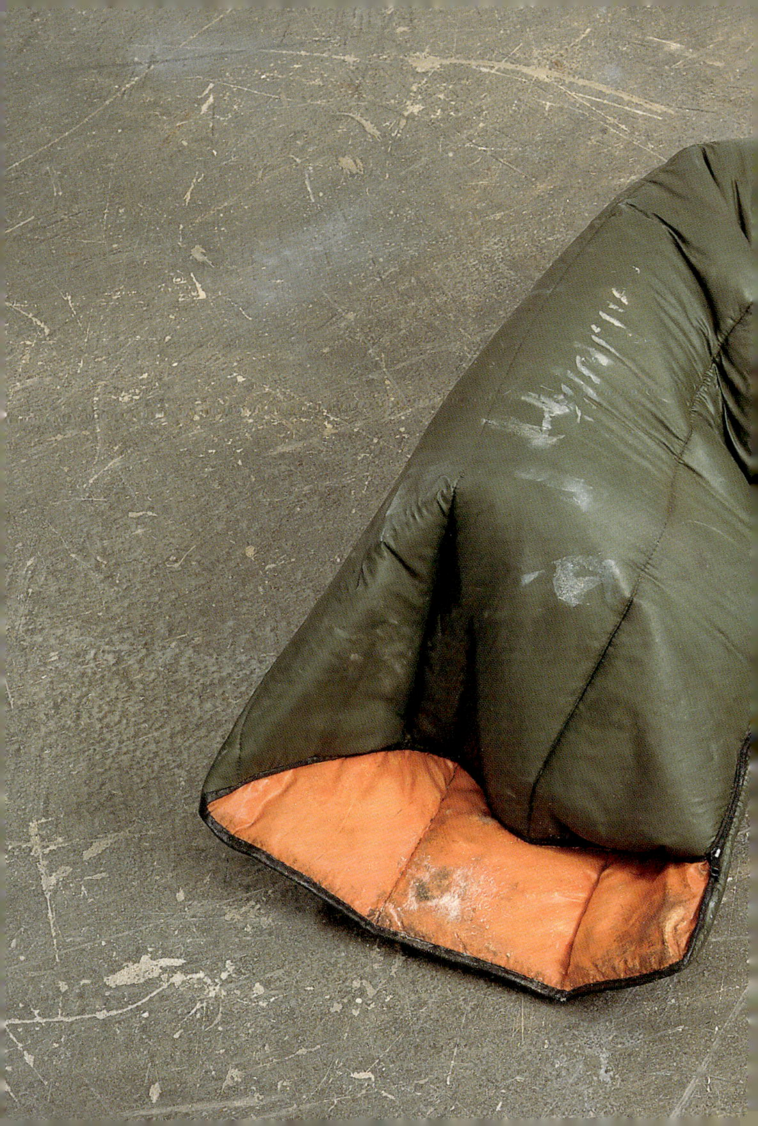

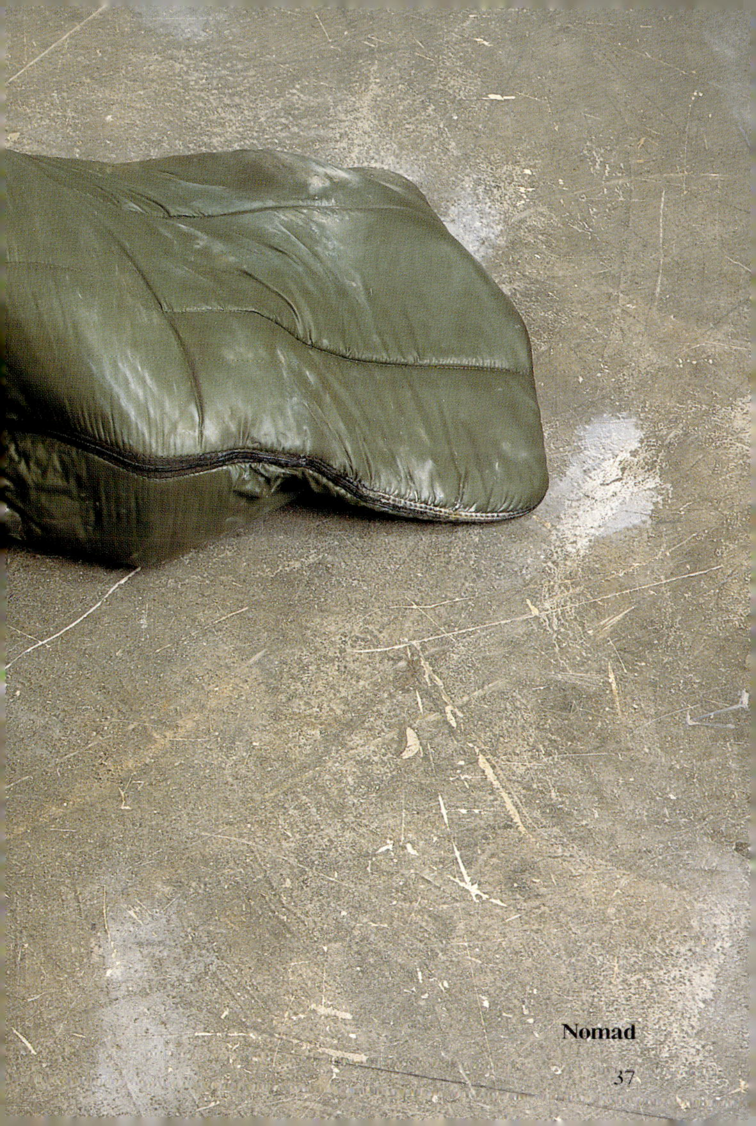

Nomad

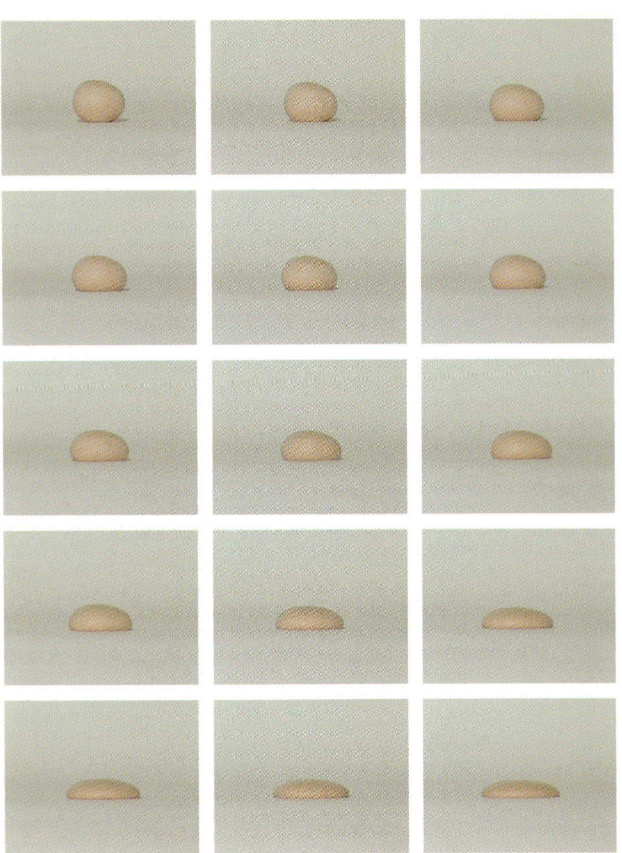

**Transmogrification (video stills)**

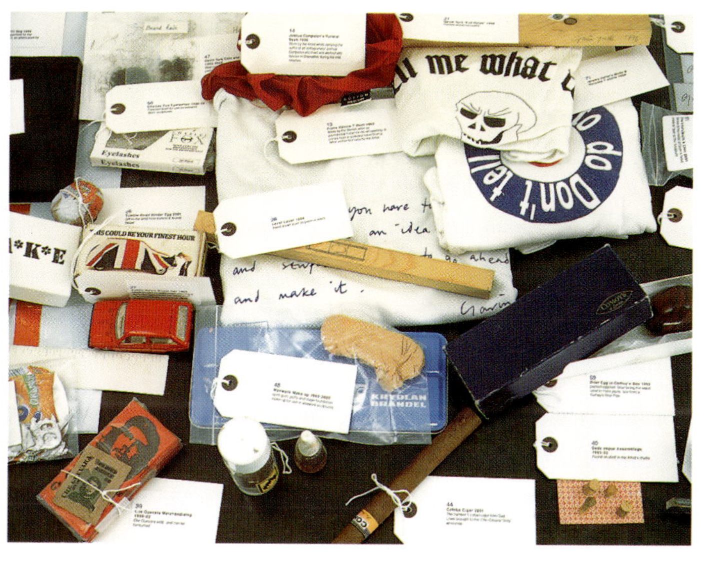


**Gavin Turk Museum (detail)**

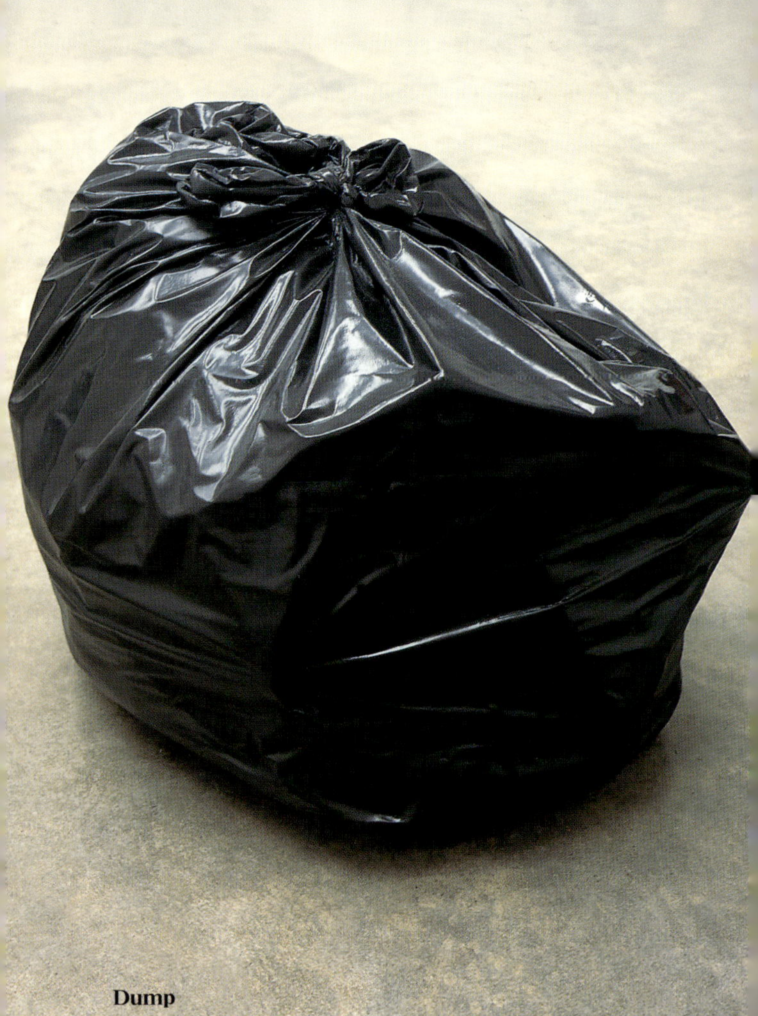

**Dump**

# ARTWORK NOTES

9
## Cave
1991
Ceramic plaque
Diameter: 49 cm
Turk's final graduation exhibition at the Royal College of Art, London, consisted of a ceramic plaque mounted on the wall of his otherwise empty studio space. The English Heritage-style blue plaque read: 'Borough of Kensington, Gavin Turk, Sculptor, worked here 1989-1991'. While what it said was quite true, the form of the plaque suggested that Turk was an important, deceased historical figure, rather than an art student simply allocated that studio. The title, 'Cave', refers to the Greek philosopher Plato's allegorical story of a group of prisoners in a cave who mistake the shadows cast on their wall for the real world itself. Plato's suggestion is that there exists another, perfect world, and that our world is just a pale shadow of this ideal.

10
## Title
1990
Pigment on canvas
183 × 274 cm
Produced while studying at the Royal College, this was Turk's first signature-based work. Being a student at the time, his signature was worth little in the art world and, as the artist's signature was brazenly the painting's only subject, Turk expected some viewers to take exception to such a provocative artwork. To counter these reactions, Turk made the work from recycled materials and employed a medieval string-and-peg process to stretch the canvas, avoiding staples and environmentally damaging adhesives. He even planted a tree to replace the recycled timber. The construction process was explained on a small label sewn onto the canvas: nobody could criticize the work for being a waste of resources. In essence, the piece took nothing from the world and gave nothing back, except the artist's labour.

12
## pipe
1991
Painted bronze and vitrine
149 × 34 × 34 cm
This painted bronze cast of a liquorice pipe sits on a plinth under a glass case. The work relates to the Belgian Surrealist René Magritte's famous painting of a pipe, 'The Treachery of Images', 1929, which has the phrase 'Ceci n'est pas un pipe' (This is not a pipe) written under it – the point being that it is not a pipe; it is a painting of a pipe. Certainly Turk's work employs a similar rebuttal, but there is another famous artwork that this piece refers to: in 1888 Vincent van Gogh made a painting of his pipe resting on the

seat of his chair. Turk used the relative scale of the chair to the pipe to determine the size of his glass vitrine, and even placed his pipe on the plinth at the same odd angle that van Gogh had placed his pipe on the chair.

13

## Window

1991

Degree show invitation card

15 × 10 cm

This postcard accompanied Turk's degree exhibition (where he exhibited 'Cave'). The image is based on the front page of the British tabloid The Sun, which, on the eve of the first Gulf War in 1991, superimposed the head of a British soldier onto the Union Jack. Its headline ran: 'Support our boys and put this flag in your window'. Turk replaced the squaddie's head with his own, so that the beret referred to artists rather than soldiers. At the time the British media were notoriously hostile to 'modern' art, and Turk couldn't resist suggesting that the press might promote artists as positive national symbols as much as they support the military.

14

## Epiphany

1992

Permanent marker on surveillance mirror

Diameter: 63 cm

'The Arnolfini Portrait', painted by the Dutch master Jan van Eyck (and often thought to depict a wedding), is famous for featuring a convex mirror in which van Eyck himself can be seen. Above the mirror the artist has written 'Jan van Eyck was here 1434'. Many think the artist was employed as witness to a marriage, with his newly invented oil-painting technique being used to create legal documentation, like photographs are today. Meanwhile, 'Epiphany' is also the title of the British Pop artist Richard Hamilton's circular, 1964 painting that bears the text 'SLIP IT TO ME': a phrase that suggests illegal activities when related to a surveillance mirror. Because Turk's piece reflects the whole room, it has the effect of adding his signature to everything around it, laying claim to all work on display with the pseudo-legal authority of van Eyck's signature.

15

## Gavin Turk Right Hand and Forearm

1992

Silkscreen on paper

86 × 68 cm

This photographic work depicts Turk's arm as if it were a pickled museum specimen – in the same way that Albert Einstein's brain has famously been preserved. 'The hand of the artist' is a much-used phrase in the art world, particularly when authenticating artworks; almost anything touched by a 'blue-chip' artist has significant economic value. And because most people relate the right hand to creative endeavours, Turk played up the idea that his right hand was that of a recognized master (even though he is actually left-handed).

17
## Pop
1993
Waxwork and vitrine
279 × 115 × 115 cm
One of Turk's most famous sculptures, this self-portrait waxwork presents the artist impersonating punk icon Sid Vicious of the Sex Pistols performing the song 'My Way' in the film 'The Great Rock 'n' Roll Swindle'. The pose Turk adopts is taken from a Hollywood publicity photograph of Elvis Presley dressed as a cowboy shooting from the hip, although this image is better known as the source for Andy Warhol's 1964 artwork, 'Triple Elvis'. The figure, which Turk wanted to look clearly like a waxwork rather than a real person, is placed in a museum case. Here, the tragic young English anarchist mimics the ill-fated American king of rock and roll, while Turk himself references Warhol, the American master of Pop art.

18
## Briar Egg
1993
Painted egg and vitrine with fluorescent light
46 × 45 × 32 cm (Egg size: Class A)
This sculpture is a blown egg, hand-painted to appear as if it has been carved from briarwood – which comes from the root-ball of the briar bush and is traditionally used to make pipes. Wood grain is a common motif in so-called 'trompe-l'œil' paintings, where the skill of the artist literally 'fools the eye' into believing that the flat depictions are in fact three-dimensional objects. Stone and wooden eggs are popular as contemplative ornaments (being elegant sculptural forms), while Turk is interested in the paradox of originality that the egg motif commonly stands for.

19
## A Night Out with Gavin Turk
1993
Performance
Turk organized this event – in collaboration with art dealer and curator William Ling – in a South London public house, gaining sponsorship from various companies and individuals for the construction of an elaborately designed exhibition stand that was erected in the bar for the evening. The event consisted of nothing more than sponsors having their support for the arts documented by being photographed with Turk on the platform. The locals were somewhat bemused by this well-attended evening; it had all the trappings of a celebrity publicity event, but no apparent purpose.

20
## Identity Crisis
1994
Screen print and light box
172 × 112 cm
In this amusingly prescient artwork, Turk mocked-up a fake

cover of HELLO! magazine and displayed it on an advertising light box. The work foresaw how the complexities of an artist's practice can be lost when they are used to feed a mainstream appetite for gossip, lifestyle and celebrity. Turk produced this piece before the mass media embraced the 'Brit Art' phenomenon and began to focus on the personalities of its most successful artists.

21
## The Spirit of Gavin Turk
1994
Bronze
27 × 10 × 10 cm
Turk created this piece – a small, bronze self-portrait resembling the Oscar statuette – as an annual prize for the person he felt most captured the 'Spirit of the Artist'. Turk launched the prize in a pseudo-ceremony at the opening of a group exhibition, 'Le Shuttle', in Berlin in 1994. Although the first award notionally went to the British artist Michael Craig-Martin, he never actually received the statuette, and the award was never presented again (Turk may yet revive the award and present it retrospectively). One of the esoteric references in this work is an unrealized project by the Italian artist Piero Manzoni: he intended to fix a gallery door closed and hang a sign on it reading 'In here is the spirit of the artist'.

22
## Pimp
1996
Painted steel
184 × 373 × 184 cm
With its perfect black-gloss finish, this high-sided skip looks more like a minimalist sculpture or giant toy than something from a construction site. Which perhaps explains its title; the clichéd image of a pimp is of someone whose snappily flamboyant style of dress is a result of an overblown sense of self-importance and power, which is ironic given their actual vocation.

24
## One thousand, two hundred and thirty four eggs
1997
Eggshell on canvas
132 × 221 cm
This is a later signature piece, with Turk's name nibbled out of white eggshells. The work references not only Manzoni's 'Achrome' paintings – textured white canvases – but also the Belgian Surrealist Marcel Broodthaers, who made a series of paintings consisting of eggshells fixed to canvas.

26
## PK2
1998
Resin and cellulose paint
58 × 50 × 26 cm
Turk has made many artworks using chewing-gum, and this piece is from a series of large, manufactured blobs that attach to the gallery wall. Another work from the same series is titled 'Stucco', playing on the fact that,

while gum literally gets stuck to street furniture, 'stucco' itself is a kind of fine plaster used for the ornate mouldings that you find in old buildings.

27
## Portrait of something that I'll never really see
1997
C-type photograph
90 × 90 cm
This photograph shares formal characteristics with the work of several recent German photographers who produce large-scale, frontal portraits against blank backgrounds. Unlike these other images, though, Turk's work is a self-portrait, showing the artist with his eyes closed: viewers can scrutinize the minutest detail of his face, but his death-mask visage gives little away. Although the title states that Turk is never able to see himself with his eyes closed, other viewers also come away with the feeling that they haven't really seen the artist; the fine detail in the photograph has revealed nothing of the subject.

28
## Droste Effect
1998
C-type photograph
22 × 90 cm
Guests at the opening of Turk's solo exhibition at the South London Gallery in 1998 found that the artist had covered all of the works with linen dustsheets for the evening. Turk had effectively made a one-night exhibition inviting the audience to take a look at their own expectations, and responses ranged from wry enjoyment to outright indignation. 'Droste Effect' is a panoramic image of the covered exhibition, and was itself included among the covered works – an apparent impossibility; how could the photograph be on the wall while it was being taken? The work's title comes from a Dutch cocoa powder, Droste, which features on its tin a picture of a nun carrying a tray with a tin of Droste, which in turn has the same picture of the nun... and on into infinity.

30, 31
## The Last Bum
1999
Waxwork
167 × 70 × 70 cm
In 1997, London's Royal Academy of Arts hosted 'Sensation', an exhibition of work by young British artists from the collection of Charles Saatchi. This highly publicized exhibition opened with a celebrity-filled party and Turk, who was exhibiting, arrived dressed as a homeless person wearing 'worn-in' clothes and a pair of specially fabricated 'shoes'. Turk said, 'I thought everyone else would be dressing up and I didn't have any party clothes, so I ended up making some'. This outfit became part of the sculpture 'Bum' – a kind of degenerate version of 'Pop'. Turk later made two similar waxworks, 'Another Bum' and 'The Last Bum'.

32

## Death of Marat

1998

Mixed media and vitrine

200 × 250 × 170 cm

This is a sculptural recreation of Jacques-Louis David's 1793 painting of the same name. David was a neo-classical painter who helped swing public opinion for the French revolution. Jean-Paul Marat was a revolutionary martyr who was stabbed to death while writing in the bath (he suffered from a skin disease that was soothed by bathing). In this version, however, Marat is replaced by a waxwork of Turk himself posed in a mirror-image of the original painting. Wax figures were first popularized by Madame Tussaud, who began her career as an art instructor to the French royal family guillotined in the revolution. Tussaud won favour with the revolutionaries by modelling wax replicas of her former masters' severed heads, and even made a waxwork of Marat the same year that David produced his painting.

33

## Death of Che

2000

Waxwork and mixed media

130 × 255 × 120 cm

Alberto Korda's famous 1960 photograph of Cuban revolutionary hero, Che Guevara, has come to stand for revolution in all its forms. A second famous image of Che, on which Turk's 'Death of Che' is based, was taken in 1967 by the CIA-led Bolivian troops that executed him. For this photograph the soldiers dressed Che's dead body in his military fatigues and propped up his head to mimic the Korda image. In Turk's recreation, the artist plays the role of the revolutionary martyr, connecting the political use of Che's image with that of Marat's in his previous waxwork, 'Death of Marat'.

34

## Œuvre (Wild Turkey)

2002

Painted fibreglass

Height: 210 × Diameter: 135 cm

Turk has produced several of these large forms, based on the eggs of different bird species. The first of these works was commissioned for the 2001 exhibition 'DEAD', organized by the artist-led group Welfare State International. The exhibition explored alternative, celebratory approaches to the taboo of death, and each artist was invited to create non-traditional versions of the cultural trappings that surround death. Turk created 'Coffin', later retitled 'Œuvre'. The collective title of the subsequent series of giant birds' egg sculptures – 'Œuvre (Hen)', 'Œuvre (Duck)', etc. – plays on the similarity between the word for the life's work of an artist, 'œuvre', and the French word for egg, 'oeuf'.

36

## Nomad

2002

Painted bronze

42 × 105 × 169 cm
After completing this painted bronze sculpture of a figure in a sleeping bag, Turk initially felt uncomfortable about showing it in a gallery context, and so placed it in a doorway opposite his central-London studio. Very few of the passers-by recognized it as being anything other than a real rough sleeper and walked quickly past. The few that did were bewildered, amazed and shocked, and looked around for an audience to their discovery. Even in a gallery the sculpture provokes strange reactions; the desire to study the work in detail is instinctive and at odds with the acquired cultural response to look away.

38
**Transmogrification**
2002
DVD
11 minutes
This screen-based work shows an egg appear to melt over a period of eleven minutes. It is unclear to the viewer whether the footage is computer-generated or has actually been filmed – the digital-video format compounds this ambiguity. In fact the footage has been filmed; the 'egg' is made from children's Crazy Putty.

39
**Gavin Turk Museum**
Ongoing
Mixed media
Dimensions variable
This 'selection of artefacts, papers, drawings, archeological samples and other ephemera from the artist's studio and various fabrication workshops' (as Turk describes it), came out of a collaboration with the Interpretation Department of the New Art Gallery Walsall for Turk's 2002 exhibition, 'Copper Jubilee'. The museum consists of several wood-and-glass display cases, each containing labelled objects relating to either the inspiration behind Turk's artworks or the process of making them. The artist describes this piece as 'showing his workings', as if the collection should be seen as a three-dimensional scrap- or sketchbook.

40 and front cover
**Dump**
2004
Painted bronze
Approximately 43 × 61 × 47 cm
Turk has made two series of painted-bronze sculptures taking the form of street rubbish: one a set of filled black bin bags, the other based on plain cardboard boxes. The art world antecedent of this construction technique is 'Painted Bronze', a 1960 sculpture by the American Pop artist Jasper Johns that took the form of two beer cans. While the boxes relate to the work of another Pop artist – Warhol and his 'Brillo' sculptures – Turk chose bin bags because they appear anonymous, even though the rubbish they contain is often highly personal.

# FURTHER READING


**Curtis, Deborah**, 'Gavin Turk in the House: A Reader', Open House, Sherborne, UK, 2003

**Live Stock Management** (eds.), 'Copper Jubilee: Gavin Turk', The New Art Gallery Walsall, UK, 2002

**Turk, Gavin**, 'The Che Guevara Diary', The Times, UK, 22 Jan, 2001

**Stallabrass, Julian**, 'High Art Lite', Verso, London, 1999

**Bradley, Alexandra, Vicky Hayward, Robert Timms** (eds.), 'Young British Art: The Saatchi Decade', Booth-Clibborn Editions, London, 1999

**Bevan, Roger**, 'Now It's My Turn to Scream: Works by Contemporary British Artists from the Logan Collection', San Francisco Museum of Modern Art, USA, 1999

**Buck, Louisa**, 'Best of 1998', Artforum, Dec, 1998

**Burrows, David** (ed.), 'Who's Afraid of Red, White & Blue?: Attitudes to Popular and Mass Culture, Celebrity, Alternative and Critical Practice and Identity Politics in Recent British Art', Article Press and UCE, Birmingham, UK, 1998

**Withers, Rachel**, 'Gavin Turk: South London Gallery', frieze, no.43, 1998

**Burrows, David**, 'Exquisite Corpses', Art Monthly, no.221, 1998

**Freedman, Carl, Gavin Turk**, 'Making Omelettes', Modern Painters, Autumn, 1998

**Compston, Joshua, Alex Farquharson**, 'Gavin Turk: Collected Works 1994-98', Jay Jopling, London / South London Gallery, 1998

**Smithard, Paula**, 'Interview: Gavin Turk', everything, 1998

**Buck, Louisa**, 'UK artist Q & A', The Art Newspaper, no.84, 1998

**Buck, Louisa**, 'Moving Targets: A User's Guide to British Art Now', Tate Gallery Publications, London, 1997

**Adams, Brooks, Lisa Jardine, Martin Maloney, Norman Rosenthal, Richard Shone**, 'Sensation: Young British Artists from the Saatchi Collection', Royal Academy of Arts, London, 1997

**Collings, Matthew**, 'Transformer Man', The Guardian, UK, 18 Oct, 1995

**Garnett, Robert**',Young British Artists IV', Art Monthly, no.187, 1995

**Kent, Sarah**, 'Shark Infested Waters: The Saatchi Collection of British Art in the 90s', Zwemmer, London, 1994

**Roberts, James**, 'Last of England', frieze, no.13, 1993

**Wilson, Andrew, Simon Bill**, 'Collected Works 1989-1993', Gavin Turk / Jay Jopling, London, 1993

**Wilson, Andrew**, 'London Summer Round-Up', Art Monthly, no.159, 1992

'Gavin Turk', frieze, no.1, 1991